REAL AS F*CK GUIDE

FOR NEW REAL ESTATE AGENTS

JULIE CHIN

Real As F*ck Guide For New Real Estate Agents
© 2023 by Julie Chin

ISBN (Print): 978-1-66789-388-4
ISBN (eBook): 978-1-66789-389-1

You passed the Real Estate Exam,

now what?!@#%

INTRODUCTION

Before I entered real estate, I had spent over 20 years as a stay-at-home mom. Then, in 2013, I found myself in the middle of a highly emotional divorce. Earning an income on my own was a foreign concept to me — I had spent much of my adult life homeschooling my three daughters, spending every day teaching, cleaning and cooking. When it came to making a resume, my professional qualifications at the time were hardly impressive for a 50-year-old woman — although when it came to juggling 3 different kiddo personalities and learning styles and sneakily eating chocolate without being caught, I was an expert! As scared as I was about the prospect of standing on my own financially, it wasn't enough for me to remain in an unfulfilling relationship for the sake of financial security. I'm sure some of you share the same feelings I felt at the time: "Am I being a dumbass?"

I didn't know where to begin, but still, I heard my mom's distant rhetoric in my head saying a woman NEEDS an education. At 46, I was embarrassed to find myself uneducated, unprepared and overwhelmed by the idea of being the oldest student in school that it took me nearly two years to get the courage to enroll at the local college. Finally, at the end of 2014, I made the call. I was filled with trepidation as I reached for the door knob to enter this scary new world. But the counselor I sat down with during my first appointment at school quickly made me feel comfortable and even excited for my new adventure. After two hours, I left the appointment enrolled in my first classes and with a deep belief in myself that I could do it! Suddenly, I didn't feel so old.

I'll spare you the drama of emotion and tears that came with trying to learn how to use the school's latest and greatest technology for the first time. Let's just say my teenager was my tutor and cheerleader, always ready with a "Mom, you've got this!" I didn't share her optimism, but she believed in me enough for the both of us. In 2018, at the age of 50, I completed college with a 3.98 GPA, adorned in honor tassels, as my daughters proudly watched as I received my degree in psychology.

On such a high, I made calls looking for employment. I was finally ready to make my own way and earn my own money. But then reality set in — I learned the going hourly rate in my field was $10.50 per hour. What the hell?! My daughter was working at Michael's Craft store for more than that. I called the school counselor to formulate a plan. She told me I would need a master's degree if I wanted to start my own practice, and in turn, make a higher wage.

"Fine," I thought. "Sign me up so I can get this done!"

Unfortunately, you need actual work experience before you can enter their masters program, she said, which of course, I didn't have. As a single mom of three trying to figure out how to be self-sufficient, the last thing I had time for was gaining experience at $10.50 an hour! At that moment, it felt like all my hard work during three years of schooling was for nothing. Not to mention all the money I had spent.

During this same time period, I was slow to learn that I couldn't keep up the lifestyle the kids and I were accustomed to. Drowning in over $100,000 in debt, I realized I had no choice but to face my children. Full of shame and absolute humiliation, I fessed up and let them know that all the trips and shopping we had been enjoying since the divorce had begun had all been piling up on credit cards. Even though I didn't have the money, I was trying to "normalize" life for my kids in an attempt to not add additional stress or changes to their lives, regardless of the consequences. I've always been a planner, but I seriously had no idea how the hell was I going to ever get myself out of this hole I dug. And it felt like the walls of the hole were caving in. The "mom guilt" was suffocating, and life was about to change even more for my sweet kiddos. And they'd already gone through so much during the four-year divorce.

It was time to go back to the drawing board. In 2017, I had taken a three-month real estate course on top of my college courses, but I was so afraid of the exam that I never took it.

Fortunately, after completing college, I found the confidence to face the exam. I passed the national exam on my first attempt, but failed the state portion. Undeterred, I went home, immediately signed up to take it again, and studied my ass off.

When I passed the real estate exam in 2018, the short-lived excitement over my accomplishment was soon forgotten, instead replaced with uncertainty about how to do the job. Clueless and desperate, I forged ahead, determined to make this work. Some thought I was too shy to be able to succeed, but inside I knew even if I did it slowly, I would figure out a way — failure wasn't an option. A few weeks after I passed the exam, I excitedly got ready to attend my first brokerage meeting. While it wasn't easy to walk in alone without knowing anyone, I knew I needed to push through my nerves. I found a seat at a table with five other agents and listened to them discussing the market. Across from me sat a tall, brown-haired, seemingly seasoned agent.

"How does a new agent go about getting customers or clients?" I asked her, my hands beginning to sweat out of fear of asking a foolish question.

"You'll figure it out, just like we had to," she responded curtly, chuckling about her snarky remark.

I had been hoping for a sense of camaraderie and support. Instead, I felt deflated and frustrated. As I searched for answers during my first few months as a real estate agent, it became clear that there wouldn't be a tremendous amount of support from other agents.

At that point, I had no backup plan and I had always been acutely aware that my girls were watching me, learning from my actions instead of my words. Learning to stand on my own two feet has been one hell of a journey. Not only did I claw my way out of debt, but I learned how to bust my ass, hustling from one house showing to another. My children have watched me struggle and overcome multiple times in multiple areas. I'm so f*%#-ing PROUD of that. Hopefully, my struggles and perseverance will serve as a road map for my children should they need the courage and strength to push into uncharted territory. At 55, I feel like I'm just beginning! Thanks to my new career in real estate, I own my own home and have very proud kiddos and happy clients. My team is growing and my new agents are gaining more confidence by the day. It's an immense joy for me to watch them grow and succeed.

Together, we can get through this. You will need to become comfortable being uncomfortable. Anything new has its learning curve, and this guide along with our online community will help you navigate the process more easily.

During my first year, I closed on $1 million in properties, despite not starting until autumn, after completing six months of training courses (really, just procrastinating). My productivity increased to $3 million the following year. By my second full year as a real estate agent, I branded my own business, Rock Star Luxe, and sold over $10 million worth of properties. By my third year, I had a team of five agents, and by my fourth, I brought on a transaction coordinator (TC) and a full-time executive assistant. To date, I've only brought new agents on to my team. I love being a mentor and being their support system so that when they find themselves sitting across from an agent who tells them they'll figure it out, they know I'm here to help them with that process.

Thank you from the bottom of my heart for putting your trust in me. xo

I've got you.

Julie Chin (Jules)

Note of Thanks

Thank you to my girls for always believing in me and supporting me. Thank you to JT for worrying behind the scenes and wanting the best for me always. To my team at Rock Star Luxe at KWCLM, your support, trust and faith in me means the world. To W, thank you for believing in me, reading the book multiple times during writing and cheering me on. To Tone, my lifelong friend, distance changes nothing, support and love and the loudest cheerleader on the planet. Thank you. Thank you to April & Buck for believing in my concept and helping to create it. I appreciate the months of long hours from both of you more than you'll ever know.

DISCLAIMER

Be aware that each state has its own rules and regulations—this guide is simply a shortcut hack and is in no way law. It's simply a book of opinion and is intended only for helpful direction.

REAL AF SECTIONS

WHAT DOES A REAL ESTATE AGENT DO?

With shows like Million Dollar Listing and Buying Beverly Hills on online streaming services, everyone thinks they have a clear idea of what the life of a real estate agent is like. Female agents get ready for their day after choosing from a wardrobe of stylish runway clothes and five inch heels before hopping into their Lamborghinis to head to showings of beautifully decorated homes, complete with flowing champagne and trendy appetizers.

While that might be one version (the version curated solely for entertainment purposes, enjoyed by those who are not and have never been a Realtor), it certainly was not my reality. My first showing was anything but Netflix-worthy. In reality, it would've been better suited for the comedy channel or a Saturday Night Live skit. And that might be giving it too much credit.

It was a brisk autumn morning in 2018, and I found myself sitting in my black Equinox an hour from home, scrolling through Facebook as I waited for the buyer, who I had agreed to pick up. My eyes kept darting towards the clock, which seemed to be frozen in time. My nerves grew over concerns about my first showing, additionally fueled by frustration over the buyer's tardiness. As someone who likes to show up everywhere at least ten minutes early, I wasn't in a great headspace.

When the buyer finally pulled in next to me, I noticed a furry friend with long, matted, white hair curled up in her arms. As she approached my car and opened the door, a breeze blew into my car, covering the jet-black interior with white dog hair. In an effort to not offend my first customer, I kept my mouth shut. During the drive to the showing, I did my best to hide my annoyance about the dog shedding all over my new car, distracting myself with small talk, which continued uninterrupted until a small rock put a crack in my windshield—the cherry on top of my first showing as an agent.

"Maybe this isn't for me," I thought to myself.

The day got progressively worse, and skepticism about my career choice replaced any optimism that existed just a day prior. Deflated by the events of the day and completely exhausted, I thought to myself that things could only get better from there.

Since then, I've had highs where I've had the opportunity to give clients news that made them shout with joy, and lows that have brought me to tears, like when I had to let a client know their offer wasn't accepted on their dream home or when a client drove over five hours one way to view a home with me and I couldn't get the lockbox open!

There are so many facets to this job. There is virtually no limit on what may be needed or asked of us, but our income is also unlimited, which makes this job an amazing opportunity for you and your family. Not to mention, it's all worth it when you experience the joy and happiness that is possible with one family after another.

Obscure tasks real estate agents have done for clients

- Used their personal carpet cleaner at a clients house
- Showed up with their truck to pack up things the sellers could not fit in their moving truck
- Re-homed a client's pet cat
- Paid for a septic location service because the buyer and seller refused and they didn't want the deal to fall apart
- Shoveled a path to the door so the buyers could enter
- Served as a marriage counselor/mediator
- Pulled weeds, trimmed trees, and mowed lawns
- Unclogged a dirty toilet
- Fed hamsters
- Crawled under a manufactured home looking for a serial number
- Sat in court on behalf of a client

- Chased squatters out of vacant homes
- Drove a client's dogs around so the house could be shown
- Helped a client escape a domestic abuse situation
- Returned mail and boxes to a seller who moved hours away
- Cleaned a client's home for three hours when the cleaner canceled at the last minute
- Took a client to rehab
- Babysat a client's kids
- Pressure washed the driveway and sidewalk of an absentee owner listing
- Dog poop…need I say more?!
- Scraped paint off the exterior siding to prepare it for the painters
- Glued shingles to the roof
- Replaced light bulbs
- Chased down a seller to get the keys while the buyer's movers waited in the driveway
- Took a client to the hospital and waited during her surgery before taking her back home
- Saged a property for ghosts
- Changed out batteries in smoke detectors

Do you see anything on the above list that the exam and real estate school prepared you for?

The real estate industry can throw anything at agents at any time. Once, at a walk-through the morning of closing, I arrived at my client's home only to find an enormous amount of personal belongings that were left behind. When I asked the client if they were returning to get their things, they let me know they didn't plan on it, drawing from the incorrect assumption that the buyers would want the items. I've heard the saying "one man's trash is another man's treasure" before, but I think this client may have taken it a step too far — especially since the "one man's trash" was dumped straight into the other man's lap. In an attempt to avoid a delayed or canceled closing—which can be the result if a home isn't as the buyer expects it—I began shoving everything into my car. With the help of some friends with trucks, we got the house to an acceptable state. And I even had enough time to wipe my sweat and look presentable!

As real estate agents, we must accept a fluid job description. Our responsibilities and the number of hours we work each week are constantly changing. Successful agents do what they need to do to help a client in need, get the job done, and keep things moving on time.

What it takes to do this job

Despite the challenging and obscure tasks we often must endure as agents, there are some basic responsibilities and skills that we all must be comfortable with. There may be a learning curve of course, but there is a plethora of training videos and information online to aid in the learning process.

Clerical/office

- General data entry, including creating, organizing, and maintaining your database and being somewhat proficient with a computer.
- Setting appointments for buyers and sellers while calculating in time for viewing as well as drive time between properties.
- You will be responsible for tracking deadlines and staying in touch not only with your clients but also with the title company, lawyers and lenders in addition to the co-broke agent.
- Every day there are tons of phone calls to make and receive, not to mention, handling emails and texts to clients, co-broke agents, leads, lenders, title companies and attorneys
- Another responsibility you will have is arranging inspectors, contractors, septic companies, showings, open houses, walk throughs and tracking down non-responsive agents.
- Prior to showings you will print the necessary paperwork for clients.

Learned skills

- It is advantageous to be an effective problem solver as issues come up with almost every deal.
- Communicating clearly with clients will save you headaches and miscommunications. It's best to make sure clients have a clear understanding of the real estate process whether they are on the list side or the buy side.
- Learning how to handle legal documents and contracts effectively and thoroughly will save your client and keep you out of trouble with the real estate commission!
- Utilizing time management skills effectively can increase your sales because you can focus your time on money making activities such as lead generation.
- Working to excel in self-accountability and self-motivation is best to achieve and complete daily objectives.

Customer service

- You will assist clients/customers with contracts and state forms.
- Referring clients to lenders, attorneys and title companies is standard in any deal. Be sure to give client's multiple choices when referring to those affiliates.
- Part of customer/client service is to be the client's protector and having their best interests in the forefront at all times.
- Presiding over negotiations is part of every deal and can be quite fun, albeit stressful occasionally.

- Creating and maintaining a follow-up system for remaining in contact with all leads and clients will ultimately bring you more business. It's a good idea to keep up with this everyday.
- Lead generation and finding customers and clients to work with is a constant task that should be time blocked to occur every day.

Technology

- Learning and handling social media marketing as well as creating and uploading posts is critical to keeping you relevant and in front of your database so that they think of you when they have a real estate need.
- Creating effective advertising and choosing the right platform medium for you and your clients will aid in awareness of your services and the listings you have been hired to sell.
- Using a signing program like Dotloop or Docusign (there are others as well) helps to keep the documents in one location and makes it easier for your clients to simply "click and sign".
- Learning to use customer management programs to organize and track your database will take hours of tasks off your "to-do" list weekly as the systems offer automated options so it can be working for you while you are out showing properties.

- Learning your area's MLS is a first and critically important step on your learning list as you need to know how to navigate and utilize this program to look up properties as well as send clients documents and listings.

On the run

- Attending appointments with potential buyers and sellers to view homes and coordinate the route settings is a time consuming "on the run" activity that will bring you closer to your ultimate goal of going under contract and getting to the closing table.
- Organizing and working open houses will assist you in getting your name out there, helps to promote the sellers home and gets you buyer leads.
- You definitely will be running around putting up for sale and open house signs unless you hire a sign install company.
- Attending networking meetings and events in your local area will keep you on the go, but will also help you to meet others in the community who could use your services.
- Walking land with clients regardless of weather and pest conditions will keep you active and out in the fresh air. It's wise to keep boots and bug spray in your car as both will come in handy.

Business planning

- Building a network of reliable professionals such as a photographer, inspector, attorney, lender, title company, handyman/woman, electrician, plumber, contractors, pressure washer, painters and general contractors will make you more valuable as a go to resource for your clients.
- Setting goals to help keep you accountable is an important first step. These can be monthly, quarterly and annually and should include a financial target for gross commission income (GCI) as well as a target number of closings to aim for. Additionally, it's a good idea to outline how many clients and customers you want to connect with. Don't forget to track your progress to ensure you reach all your goals!
- Reserving income to hold you over until you start having closings could save you enormous stress.

CHOOSING THE RIGHT BROKERAGE

When I signed up for real estate school in the spring of 2017, a woman named Erika, reached out to me to speak about the brokerage she worked for. At the time, I didn't know that her job was to recruit new agents—I simply liked her vibe and appreciated the valuable information she was providing me about being an agent and the available training the brokerage provided. I had completed the real estate course that June, but did not take the exam until the next year due to the time consuming college courses I was enrolled in, at the young age of 50.

The truth is, I was afraid of taking the exam, so I procrastinated and focused all my energy on my last two college semesters. When I successfully completed my hardest and final course, statistics, despite my intense aversion to math, it gave me the confidence necessary to face the real estate exam and start focusing my energy on my soon-to-be career.

After weeks of studying my ass off, endlessly reading the sleep-inducing chapters in my study book, I passed the exam.

I excitedly texted Erika the news. The following week, we met at the office and chatted at a picnic table, the warm sun complimenting her friendly demeanor—the ideal setting for such a big decision. We spoke about what the brokerage offered, and in the end, I signed up simply because I liked her. She may have gotten me hook, line and sinker, but I'm not mad about it!

While my decision-making process has evolved since those early days, joining that brokerage ended up working out perfectly. They offered so many learning opportunities that I quickly realized that if I failed, it was on me—it certainly would not be from lack of educational opportunities.

Choosing a brokerage that is right for you should be your focus. As you meet with different brokerages, it's important to remember that you are interviewing them, not the other way around.

I got lucky with the one and only firm I sat down with, but in hindsight, I've always wondered how they compared to other brokerages at that time.

In order to fully understand what's available, you should interview at least three different brokerages. From there, you get to decide what fits with your goals, your learning style and what type of culture suits you best. You can also gain an understanding of the financial breakdown of different brokerages, such as what fees you're going to pay out of your commission. Knowing the right questions to ask a brokerage can be quite daunting and priorities vary from agent to agent, but regardless, you should walk out of each interview with an understanding of the brokerage's commission splits, culture, offerings, and what you can expect from them and vice versa. Doing as much homework as possible on the brokerage before your first interview can be extremely beneficial, and will help you have a comprehensive list of questions prepared.

Here are some things to consider when interviewing a brokerage:

Culture

- What is the mission statement of this brokerage?
- What words best describe the culture at this brokerage—does their vibe fit you?
- What is the level of involvement of this brokerage within the community (if this is important to you—some people want to be part of a brokerage that gives back to the community).

Money

- Are there any fees for using eSignature—a program necessary for allowing remote electronic signatures for contracts?
- What is the commission split? For example, what percentage of each commission do you get to keep?

- Is there a royalty fee, also known as a "franchise fee," in addition to the commission split? This typically ranges from an additional three to eight percent.
- Are there any other fees (some companies charge monthly office fees, errors and omissions insurance (E&O), an education fee, a start-up fee, a printing fee, a desk rental fee or an administrative fee, to name a few)?
- Do they offer a commission cap? This means that once you pay in X dollars of your commission and royalty for the year, you no longer have to give the brokerage their predetermined percentage. Each commission check for the remainder of that year is all yours, minus a small administrative fee.
- Are there transaction fees for each deal?
- What do newer agents usually earn in their first year and second years?

Assistance

- Does the brokerage offer office assistance with contracts or transaction coordinator (TC) services to ensure you are compliant with brokerage and state standards? TCs also track deadlines and help with communication between your client and the lender, title company and/or attorney. Are any fees involved?
- Do they have someone available daily, including evenings and weekends, to assist with questions that may arise with

a contract or a system/program? What is the response time for such questions?

- Does the brokerage have in-house legal support?
- Does the brokerage have a technology support team in place, and if so, are there any fees for using the services?

Professional Benefits

- How will joining this brokerage help you get your business off the ground and into production?
- What kind of training is available? Is it in person, online, group or one-on-one?
- Do they have a mentorship program, and if so, what does it involve and what are the associated fees (if any)?
- Do they have a list of items that the brokerage will be doing to help you acquire business?
- Do they have a list of resources they provide to help new agents?
- Do they offer buyer or seller leads to their agents, and if so, is there a fee? If they are provided, be sure to ask how they decide who gets each lead, how they are distributed, if there is a referral fee charge and where these leads are generated from. It's also important to know what percentage of leads provided typically convert into closed sales.
- Do they cover any continuing education credits, and if so, is there a fee (it's not a huge deal if they don't since your local board will offer them and there are a ton of options online)?

Check out the CE Shop for classes for all states at https://www.theceshop.com/real-estate/continuing-education

Brokerage Expectations

- Does the brokerage require agents to work at a desk, greet walk-in customers and answer any phone calls for a specific number of hours each week? This is known as "up-time" and "desk-time" among other names.
- If so, does each agent get to keep any leads acquired during mandatory desk time?
- Does the brokerage require new agents to shadow a seasoned agent?
- What training is required?

Provided Items and Services

- Does the brokerage have buyer and seller listing packets, which are typically useful for when you go to meet potential buyers and sellers, available to new agents?
- Is there a conference room available for client meetings, and if so, what is the process for an agent to reserve it? Are there any fees?
- Do they provide marketing materials (for a fee or free) such as business cards, a website, signage or headshots?
- Do they provide combination or electronic lockboxes?

- Do they have an assistance program in place with financial aid for the new agent's local board and national dues?

Technology

- Do they have a customer relationship management system (CRM) in place, and if so, are there any training courses available or associated fees? Who owns the data? If you leave the brokerage you want to be owning and remain in control of everything you input into the system.
- Do they require Dotloop, Docusign, or another specific document-signing tool or can the agent decide? Is training offered on these programs?
- Do they offer any paid-for apps, like Supra, which is an electronic lockbox, or Forewarn, which is a phenomenal safety tool allowing you to look up a person prior to meeting face-to-face to ensure they are who they say they are and if they have a criminal record?

General Considerations

- How many real estate agents are there in the brokerage or the specific office you'd be working out of?
- Are there any mandatory meetings? For example, are there monthly or weekly sales meetings or daily huddle sessions?
- Would it be possible to take a tour of the office and meet some of the agents and office staff?

- Would it be possible to sit in on an upcoming training session or brokerage meeting?
- Is the broker also an active agent? This is an important consideration because if this brokerage does offer leads, the broker will be competing with you for those same leads. This could mean the broker has an advantage over the agents and individual agents will be at a disadvantage for leads.
- What is the average turnover of agents?

Obviously, you shouldn't show up with a textbook-sized stack of questions to slide across the table to your potential future broker. But at the same time, you're not going to get answers to questions you don't ask. Don't be in a rush—you're the badass in charge here, so take the contract with you to review at your leisure.

JOINING A TEAM VS. BECOMING A SOLO AGENT

During my first full year as an agent in 2019, I entertained the idea of joining a team and began meeting and interviewing with multiple team leads to get a better idea of the advantages and disadvantages of being on a team. Interviewing with multiple teams allows new agents to get a sense of how each team operates, what they offer and which might be a better fit. As I mulled through my options, reviewing my notes from the interviews, I made a list of the pros and cons for each team which ultimately led to my decision to remain solo.

While arriving at your team interview prepared with questions is essential, there are a few benefits to both remaining solo and joining a team.

The benefits of remaining solo

- You get to create your logo, business name, website and signage choices, assuming your brokerage allows that kind of freedom. This can be quite fun and can be a very exciting process! You can design it all yourself or hire a marketing company to put their creative expertise to work for you.

- Being a solo agent means remaining accountable only to yourself and your broker.
- Working for yourself eliminates paying a double split; part to the broker and part to the team, which means more cash in your pocket!
- Not being on a team means that you get to be greedy—all the leads are yours!
- If you decide to work alone, you have the opportunity to build your own business and brand instead of a shared brand.
- You're F%$@# in control!

The benefits of joining a team

- Some teams provide lead generation. This is a benefit to you which will build your business faster and at their expense not yours.
- Operational costs of starting up your business may be covered by the team, such as business cards, signage, marketing materials, etc., which means less debt for you!
- A huge benefit if offered is training, mentorship and assistance with documents as this will get you up and running faster.
- Many teams offer support staff for various tasks like deadline alerts, contract help, follow up with affiliates as well as clients and documentation assistance.

- A huge perk to being on a team can be vacation coverage so you can travel and enjoy your personal time knowing that your teammates have your business covered for you.
- Some teams hire a person to work inside sales for the team and their focus is setting appointments for the agents, cold calling for leads, and client nurture services which can keep agents connected and busy with appointments with buyers and sellers.
- If needing accountability is your thing a team can assist by making sure you complete the tasks assigned to you.
- When everything is already so overwhelming, you know you are not left to face things alone when you're on a team.

An obvious positive to being on a team is that you will need to front less costs.

Ultimately, your final decision will come down to your overall goals and desires. Joining a team will likely provide you with leads and offer support and mentoring, but you will pay a percentage of your commission in return. To make the most informed decision possible, it's wise to not only interview the team lead, but also some of the team members. If possible, check in with someone relatively new—maybe someone who has been in the industry for only a few months—and someone who has been on the team for a few years. Follow this method with each team, as they can vary significantly.

The bottom line is to figure out what feels right for you, which might differ from what's right for someone else. It's also important to remember you're not signing your life away—if you try it and decide it's not for you, you can always leave. But of course, be sure to read and understand the terms of your contract. Seriously, read that shit.

WHAT YOU NEED TO GET STARTED

There are certain items that are simply not optional; for example, a cell phone or a printer. Attempting to work without these items would be like taking a job delivering pizzas and not having a car to drive. Like any business you might start (and that is what you're doing here), you need to spend money to make money. And it definitely ain't easy! The list of needed accouterments is extensive.

A headshot

This gives potential clients a glimpse at who you are. It doesn't have to be shot by a professional, but it should be a professionally looking image—a blurry photo from your 2002 MySpace profile won't cut it. Be intentional about your appearance and what is in the background of your photo. This picture should be somewhat close up, but not too close! It should also be a recent and accurate image of you (NO CATFISHING).

Business cards

Whether or not paper business cards are still relevant is a subject of debate. While, for many, an electronic business card will suffice, old-fashioned paper business cards allow a personal interaction as you hand it directly to someone. Hopefully your card represents your style and stands out to the recipient, making it a memorable moment. I'd advise not being creative with the sizing and shape, being as for decades, people have gotten used to a standard size and shape. A business card that doesn't fit in a wallet for example, can leave some feeling annoyed, which is the last thing you want. But you can still get creative. Try a thicker card stock, add foil or go with metal if that floats your boat. This is your business, so you do you.

A professional online presence

In today's day and age, many people's first impression of you will likely be digital. Potential leads will have done some stalking online prior to meeting you, which is why you need to have an up to date website, social media accounts and up to date information and images that fully show the world the professional image you want to share. Your online image that reflects your goals should be consistent across all platforms.

Office supplies

There is no shortage of items needed to perform all the tasks of a real estate agent, like a computer, printer, paper, ink, staples, paper clips and pens (have back up, these are items you need back stock on so you can always be fully prepared for a last minute showing).

Cell phone

Needing a cell phone is a no-brainer of course, but your big decision is whether or not to have a separate business cell phone or simply use your personal number and just carry one phone everywhere. Carrying two phones may be a hassle for some, but for others, keeping the personal number private is worth it.

WiFi

Having WiFi is just as important as having oxygen. Consider adding WiFi to your car, as this can be advantageous when writing contracts on the run or when a client is asking for property information.

Signage

There are many options and varying price points when it comes to signage. Choices can include different types of sign holders, such as metal stakes, metal frame holders or wooden posts. When it comes to the actual sign itself, there are a plethora of choices such as sign size, the material it's made from (metal, pvc, corrugated plastic), add ons like special coatings for durability, reflective material for better nighttime viewability, etc. You'll want to consider ordering sign riders and open house signs as well. If your brokerage or team provides signs, you'll save a bundle. There are many sign companies online, making it easier for you to check out your options:

https://www.buildasign.com/

https://www.deesign.com/

https://www.customrealestatesigns.com/

http://www.vistaprint.com

License and board costs

To become a REALTOR®, a real estate agent must join their local, state and national associations. These fees vary locally and by state, so check with your board and real estate commission. These are a big expense upfront, especially when you haven't even started earning any money yet.

All of these things will add up, so make sure to keep your costs in check. Keep a spreadsheet or a written list so that you can keep track of what you've spent and what the items will do for you.

When you get started, it won't be long before every company imaginable will be reaching out to get your money for their services. And chances are everything will seem necessary, and you might feel that you'll be lagging behind unless you buy it all. But before you buy that client management software or pay for lead generation, remember that their job is to make their product seem like a necessity—they want your business and money. Check with your broker and other agents if you're not sure if you can live without a specific company and what they are offering. Being selective about your costs up front will allow you to get to your first closing with less debt!

WHAT TO KEEP IN YOUR CAR

After buying all of the supplies you should keep on hand to be prepared for incidents, you might feel as if you need to attach a U-Haul to the back of your car to get it to the office!

Prior to heading out to show homes and throwing yourself completely into this new real estate agent lifestyle, be prepared for the unexpected at showings, open houses and walkthroughs. Some agents tend to keep a tool box in their car, while others won't leave the house without pepper spray or a gun. What you have with you at all times is ultimately up to you, but here are a few things you might want to consider, according to a number of experienced agents.

Clerical

- Clipboard
- Extra signs
- Business cards
- Buyer guide
- Seller guide
- State documents
- Pens
- Notebook

This list likely has no surprises on it, whereas the items on the following lists may stump you. I'd suspect carrying a toolbox isn't the first thing you'd think of when deciding to become a real estate agent; however, being prepared for the unexpected is necessary. A client might want to measure rooms to see if their furniture will fit, or they might be concerned that the floors are uneven (having a marble or tennis ball will be beneficial here). Zip ties are used often to help keep signs from blowing out of their frames or attaching them temporarily to sign posts. When getting ready for an open house, it's best to minimize any annoyances for the prospective buyers—so you'll be happy you have your WD-40 when you find a bunch of bothersome squeaky doors. Similarly, make sure you're fully-stocked with nine volt batteries, because a chirping smoke detector catapults itself to the top of the annoying items list. A ladder is another good idea, especially for height challenged agents.

Tools and such

- Tool kit
- Scissors or utility knife
- Measuring tape
- A marble or tennis ball
- WD-40
- Tape
- Zip ties
- Winter weather supplies

Personal protective equipment (PPE)

- Toilet paper
- Hand sanitizer
- Booties
- Gloves
- Masks

Other

- 9-volt batteries
- A folding chair
- Boots
- lightbulbs
- Lock boxes
- Phone charger
- Bug spray
- Water bottles and snacks
- Umbrella
- Dog treats

Safety

- Pepper spray (follow your state laws)
- First aid kit
- Tylenol
- Gun (if that is your thing and you're licensed)
- Flashlight

Clean up

- Dog shit clean up bags
- Mini broom and dustpan
- Trash bags
- Paper towel
- Hand soap
- Cleaning supplies

Some of this might sound like items you'd find in a serial killer's car on an episode of Forensic Files, but trust me, so much of it is needed and used regularly.

For example, when you spend hours showing homes and eventually need a bathroom, only to find your next showing barren with no toilet paper, you'll be thanking me for telling you to keep toilet paper in your car.

We have put an agent realAF toolkit together for your convenience, complete with a roll of toilet paper.

This can be found at www.realafprogram.com/toolkit

STEPS YOU CAN TAKE TO GENERATE BUSINESS

In the beginning, I focused on Zillow for my leads. This is a contentious topic—so many people will tell you to not buy leads. And while it did work for me, I know plenty of people that it hasn't worked for.

Purchasing leads is really only beneficial if you answer the calls as you receive them. In the beginning, I sometimes struggled to put on a cheery attitude and answer incoming calls when it interrupted something I was doing with my family. Once I realized that every missed call was a missed opportunity and potentially lost income, I picked up my phone every time. Over time, I learned to navigate the conversations and deal with rejections, eventually establishing my own business. As I built confidence, I found it easier to reach out to people I didn't know, and as my business grew, I received referrals from other agents and past clients.

While knowing how to generate business is arguably the most important knowledge you can have when becoming a real estate agent, it's not always shared among agents. But I'll let you in on a few secrets, because I want you to be a BADASS, successful agent. If there is only one topic you retain information from, this should be it—lead generation is your lifeline to future income.

"Lead generation" is a term that means finding customers/clients who need your services. In other words, generating leads!

When you enter the industry, you'll find many agents are reluctant to share ideas, tips, and tricks in an attempt to minimize competition. Because of this, entering the wonderful world of real estate can be a frustrating experience!

Selling real estate is not for the unmotivated—you can't sit on your ass and believe business will come to you. That said, there are thousands of ideas out there, proven to work by hungry, driven agents.

Door-to-door

Cue the music: someone's ringing the bell! Yes, physically walking up to people's homes and knocking on their door, introducing yourself and asking if they are interested in selling can be very effective. Some agents go to the door with marketing material, local statistics about home sales and prices, a small gift or an announcement of a nearby open house.

Phone calls

Prior to picking up the phone, make sure to check the "The Do Not Call Registry." Calling individuals on this list can land you in deep shit with the Federal Trade Commission (FTC). According to the FTC, over $178 million in civil penalties and $112 million in restitution or disgorgement has been recovered since 2003. "The Do Not Call Registry" can be found at https://www.donotcall.gov/

Begin with those you know—you have plenty of contacts in your phone already. Send out a few texts or make some calls, asking if they know anyone who might be interested in buying, selling or investing in real estate. When calling or speaking with individuals who say they don't have a real estate-related need right now, it can pay dividends to ask them if they know someone who might be interested in buying, selling or investing in real estate that they could put you in contact with.

Networking

There are a number of organizations throughout the country, like Rotary, who specifically work within the community to help residents in need. Business Network International, known as BNI, offers support and learning and is focused on in-group business referrals. Your local Chamber of Commerce connects business owners through local events. A couple others are LeTip, which focuses on supporting and nurturing strong relationships between non-competing business owners, and Mastermind Groups, which bring together like-minded peers for brainstorming, accountability and encouragement. This list could be extensive, but this will get you started. All of these groups are about connection; they have regular events or meetings, all of which will allow you to meet new people. As with anything in life, you will likely get out of it what you put into it.

- https://letip.com/
- https://www.bni.com/
- https://www.rotary.org/en
- https://www.uschamber.com/co/chambers
- https://www.meetup.com/topics/masterminds/

Volunteering

Volunteering can be a great way to meet people, connect with like-minded individuals, and get your name out there. After all, real estate is a relationship-based business—meeting and getting to know others allows them the opportunity to get to know you and trust you to handle their biggest asset.

ZIP code purchasing

Companies will send you leads in the ZIP codes you purchase to advertise in. The verdict is mixed on the effectiveness of this.

A few companies who offer this are Realtor.com, Zillow.com and Marketleader.com, among others.

Tapping your personal database

Everyone has friends, family and businesses they frequent, and reaching out to them can go a long way. Attaching your business card to a little gift bag with candies, cookies or something else (get creative!) and then bringing it to local businesses can help you stand out amongst a sea of agents. Don't forget to include contractors. This is a mutually beneficial relationship—not only can you be a source of business for them, but you can be a resource to your clients by providing contractor referrals. Obviously, it's important to do your due diligence before recommending someone, as you will be putting your reputation on the line as well.

Advertising

The most traditional way of advertising is to take an ad out in your local newspaper highlighting your areas of speciality, such as relocation, downsizing or even mentioning that you are an expert of a specific neighborhood or town.

Some real estate magazines will help you design your ad so that you can advertise your listings and open houses. As a new agent, you can also make the ad all about you and your strengths, focusing simply on what you want to specialize in such as a neighborhood or vacation homes.

Social media opens so many opportunities because there are so many platforms. You can spend virtually nothing and still get your information out there, or you can boost your posts for a predetermined fee as well as choose your demographic and locale.

Billboards can be expensive and you may or may not get calls because your face is prominently displayed on a 20-foot sign, but you can use this medium to develop your presence in that area.

Website

Making sure your site is easy to navigate is essential, as is optimizing it so that it is picked up by search engines. You can check your pages/site yourself or you can outsource and leave it to the professionals.

Build referral partnerships with other agents

But of course, make sure they don't work in your specific area, so they're more likely to send you referrals. At closing, you will share a percentage of your commission with them in exchange for the referral. Typically the amount is 20-30 percent of your side of the deal. In addition to agents in your state, build relationships with agents in other states. A great way to do this is by utilizing Facebook referral groups.

Mailers

You can send handwritten notes or postcards to homeowners in specific neighborhoods of interest. If you are in an area that is a tourist destination and popular with second home owners, consider writing letters specifically to the absentee homeowners asking if they would be interested in selling.

Develop a niche

If there is a need in your area that isn't being addressed, like someone who focuses specifically on short term or long term rentals or military housing needs, be the local expert who fills that gap. Providing information about upcoming events, seasonal activities, etc. can also solidify you as an area expert, and is a great way for you to offer value to potential clients.

Open houses

As you work towards getting your first clients, contact other agents and offer to work their open houses. Not only can this provide you with an invaluable experience ahead of your own open houses, but it can also be a great way to generate leads.

Make sure you discuss expectations in advance, including how leads will be handled, with the list agent. It's also a good idea to shadow a couple of open houses before you handle one solo. In fact, you can even start by stopping by an open house, being sure to pay attention to what the agent is and is not doing. For example, if the agent at the open house is on her phone the entire time and pays you no mind, you can check that off the list of what not to do. Contrarily, take note if the agent is friendly and knowledgeable and makes you feel welcome.

Expired & "For Sale by Owner" (FSBO) listings

An expired listing is simply a listing in which the listing agreement that was in place between the homeowner and the listing agent has expired. It is proper etiquette to first reach out to the agent and ask them if the owner plans on reinstating that contract with them.

An FSBO, or "for sale by owner" listing, can be another great lead. A person who has listed their home on their own has likely done so to avoid paying agent compensation. So your mission, should you choose to accept it, is to get them to understand why hiring you to sell their home AND compensate you for it is actually in their best interest. Also important to note is that if you have a buyer for a FSBO, you can call the home owner and ask them if they are willing to pay a buyer agency fee if you bring a buyer who purchases. So even if they aren't willing to have you list it for them, you can still potentially get the sale.

Divorce leads

This option isn't for everyone. You can contact local divorce attorneys and build a relationship with them so that they will recommend you in someone's time of need.

Estate attorneys

While we're on the topic of attorneys, estate attorneys are in touch with families who are grieving the death of a loved one and sadly, often need to sell the property. If this is a route you'd like to pursue, you can even watch the obituaries, like a morbid vulture.

Social media

Utilize your social media platforms—LinkedIn, Facebook, Instagram, Twitter, TikTok and SnapChat, for example—to connect and communicate with others. Don't forget to use Instagram stories, boosted posts, or sponsored posts. You can also post surveys to generate engagement. For example, a post that asks "What's stopping you from buying a home?" can get a lot of user engagement on your social media accounts. If you successfully make a sale or help a buyer find a home, post about it so others will begin trusting in you to help them. In this industry, it's okay to brag!

Testimonials

Always ask past clients to write a review and then post it everywhere. This helps to showcase your strengths as well as advertise your successes to your audience while simultaneously building trust and confidence in your abilities.

Farming

Farming is a marketing technique some agents use to create business in a specific area or neighborhood. With these ideas, you will have your contact information and the brokerage you work for front and center on whichever medium you choose: banners, postcards, letters, events, etc. But make sure you are compliant with not only your town and state regulations, but also your brokerage.

Emails to your database

Using programs like Mailchimp will allow you to send out monthly newsletters and bulk communications. It is also a great way to stay in touch with and keep your name in front of potential clients.

Customer relationship management (CRM)

Using a smart CRM, which allows you to set up automatic touch points—emails, newsletters and announcements—with each person, is a great way to keep your name in front of your database.

Host a first-time buyers seminar

Hosting a first-time buyer's seminar is a great way to get yourself out in front of potential buyers. If you check with your local library, they may have space that you can use for free and they will likely advertise this event for you at no cost. If your library isn't an option, get creative—ask your local coffee house or meet in the park if the weather allows. The focus should be on keeping costs at a minimum. For additional advertising, you could put an ad in your local newspaper and on social media with event information including day, time and location. Make sure you prepare your marketing information, business cards and an organized agenda of what you plan on teaching the first time homebuyer about. It is a bonus to partner with a lender for the event so that they are present to answer any questions about specific loan products, not to mention they often provide drinks and snacks.

Advertise new listings

As a real estate agent, it's our job to sell homes. And a critical part of selling something is advertisement. Don't forget to contact local news sources like newspapers, radio stations or even television channels. Utilizing social media, printing flyers and delivering them to other brokerages and businesses can be helpful. Getting coverage is a win-win for you and your seller, as it can also boost your reputation and gain you future potential clients. The focus is keeping your face and name in front of people.

Clubs

Join or start a club! The opportunities are endless here—the point is simply to get your name out there and create a network for yourself. And maybe have a little fun!

Sponsor events

Sponsoring events at places like your local humane society is a great way to make people in your town aware of your existence while simultaneously doing something positive in your community. Consider hosting or sponsoring a fundraising event for a charity you support and believe in. This is mutually beneficial, as these local non-profit organizations are always in need of sponsors. It helps them while simultaneously promoting you and your brand!

Think out of the box

For example, with permission during the holidays, you could hand out candy canes or seasonal treats with your business card attached or provide branded water bottles during a 5K event. If you're farming a neighborhood, you could leave a pumpkin at each home during autumn or a U.S. flag on every lawn for the Fourth of July, but be sure your contact information is included. Getting creative and seeing how you can present your information, provide a gift and incorporate ideas into different holidays can be a lot of fun!

Gratitude

Recognizing and remembering those who have contributed to your business growth is incredibly important and the right thing to do. Giving a handwritten card, a small gift, or a gift card can make the recipient feel appreciated. You can even host a party once or twice a year to say "thank you," which, although it's a bit more costly, can double as a networking event.

Remember to always be branded

Promoting yourself through your personalized branding is a great way for people to be reminded of who you are, what you do and associate you with your brand. Having your logo on your car, jacket, hat, shirts, sweatshirts and to-go coffee tumblers keeps your brand and service you provide in front of people.

Leverage

Believe it or not, getting help for yourself can make a huge impact when you're ready. For example, Your Realty Leverage offers everything you might need from part-time or full-time assistants to handling your social media presence to data entry, listing entry and everything contract to close! They will even handle recruiting AND training for you!

HOW TO FARM

Farming basically refers to a repetitive task you need to perform over an extended period of time. Like the traditional word "farming," which is defined as the activity of growing crops and raising livestock, real estate agents need to tend to their neighborhoods and keep their face in front of the home owners so that when they consider selling they think of you and only you.

According to Andrea Stenberg, a social media strategist, in her article titled, What is the rule of 7? And how will it improve your marketing? It's beneficial to keep your face, information and what you do in front of your target audience on a consistent basis. The old marketing adage with the "rule of seven" simply means that people don't think to take action until they see something seven times.

She further adds, "In today's world, people are being bombarded with messages constantly. It is truly difficult to get past all this noise and be heard.The first few times someone sees your message it's likely it won't completely register with them. We all have marketing blinders we've built up over time – otherwise we'd be overwhelmed with the constant noise from businesses clamoring to be heard. It's no different with your prospects.

They're not sitting around waiting for you to show up. They're busy living their lives and you may not even be a blip on their radar". Check out more about Andrea Stenberg and view her courses at http://www.TheBabyBoomerEntrepreneur.com

To combat being part of the noise, settle in and consider your farming as a one to three year experiment. Start by sending letters to homeowners in your targeted area, letting them know you have interested buyers and asking if they would like to sell. You could also send useful information such as a list of local contractors and their contact information, game schedules for popular sports teams and dates of local festivals, fairs and farmers markets. Postcards are another easy way to connect with local homeowners. Use them to offer to give a personalized home value to the owner, share the current market condition or alert them of a just listed, under contract or just sold property. A magnet with your contact information along with local government contact information, school information or simply the calendar for the year is another classic, and may linger on their refrigerator for the year. If you want to plan a social gathering that doubles as a community force for good, you could put together a local meet and greet for the neighborhood that's also a pet food collection for the local humane society or a warm coat collection for a local charity.

Ultimately farming is about being consistent and intentional— coming from a place of value and keeping your name in front of the homeowners in your chosen area. Many agents create opportunities from their own hobbies or interests, such as, launching a community garden, offering free yoga classes for beginners, organizing a neighborhood shred day or clean out clutter event. The options are unlimited. Whatever you decide to do, remember that this is a marathon not a sprint, go forward with intention.

REPUTATION

The first time I received a negative review online, I was shocked. I was about 13 months into my career when a client I'd been working with for weeks extended an invitation to take our professional relationship to a personal level. He had mentioned that he was looking forward to me coming over after the closing to enjoy his homemade wines with him. In an attempt to keep my business and personal relationships separate, I declined, which didn't sit well with him. I felt surprised and angry about his review and while there wasn't much I could do to erase the stain on the public forum, I decided to immediately reach out to clients who hadn't given me reviews previously to offset this one review.

Your reputation in any industry directly impacts the trust and confidence others will have in you. Real estate is a relationship-based business; your reputation is everything. And while mistakes happen, good communication and ethical behavior can hopefully minimize anything tarnishing our reputation.

Being ethical and professional is pretty straightforward. The Code of Ethics outlines appropriate and inappropriate methods of responding and behaving. Read it, pay attention in your continuing education unit courses (CEU) and then execute what you learned on a daily basis. Remember, we are all in this together—working for the interests of our client with a common goal of getting them to the closing table. There is no need to treat the agent on the other side of the deal as you would your spouse when you're in the middle of a divorce mediation! Real estate agents need to work together harmoniously. Some things you can do to work in this direction is to respond to notifications quickly, follow through on tasks before they are due and think before you click the send button. Feel free to use that last one in your personal life as well!

ETIQUETTE

Maintaining proper etiquette with clients, agents and affiliates really falls right in line with your reputation. This job and the situations you'll often find yourself in can be an emotional rollercoaster for all those involved.

Imagine selling the home you've lived in for decades because you have to, for some unforeseen circumstance—not because you want to. A couple going through a divorce is a commonly seen example of one of these emotionally-fueled, forced sales. The house has to be sold to accommodate a division of assets and the parties involved are likely hurting, angry and scared. In these emotionally-driven circumstances, we are often the client's confidant. And unfortunately, we don't have a suit of armor on to shield us from the emotional onslaught—we must face it and set our own emotions aside while remaining empathetic to our clients. This is a great time to remember to think before you click the "send" button on that text or email. It's our job to remain calm and level-headed, and we need to do our absolute best to refrain from jumping in a seat on the emotion-coaster.

It's also important to be weary of oversharing, not just to protect yourself, but also your clients. We've all overshared before and regretted it. In fact, I used to be as guilty as it gets when it comes to oversharing.

One night, while representing friends on the sale of their home, I mistakenly shared a text I received from the buyer's agent, and it ultimately resulted in that offer not being accepted. I should have remembered that in that moment, they were clients first and friends second. In the end, they were thrilled with the offer they accepted, but it was never my place to influence that decision.

We are not infallible, and it's important to recognize our errors and learn from them. Proper etiquette would have been to simply present the offers without the additional commentary.

So, let's tackle some etiquette pointers:

- Be your client's protector in times of stress.
- Do not overshare—think about whether your client really needs to know what you're considering telling them.
- Attempt to problem solve before running to the client. This is part of being their protector—they don't need to know all of the details, do they?
- Be polite, courteous and kind to your fellow agent as well as your clients. Respect goes a long way.
- Maintain professionalism by answering texts and emails in complete sentences. Always reference the property and

topic at hand, and include your and your brokerage's name. Agents and affiliates are all juggling a multitude of properties and variables, so you can't assume they keep it all in their head. This helps to avoid miscommunication and save everyone time.

- When you go to a showing, remember to give the listing agent feedback. It's important to always be polite, even if the place is a complete shit hole. Frankly, the agent likely already knows it's a shit hole. While constructive and honest feedback is good, you should always consider how you're wording it.

- When attending a showing with clients, remember you are entering someone's home. The buyers and their kiddos (if present) don't need to lie down on the seller's bed. Many people are okay with cabinets and closets being opened, but keep your hands off their stuff. I also wouldn't advise allowing your client to light a cigarette as you're touring a home—again, this is not good etiquette. While navigating these things with buyers can be tough, it's important when it comes to your overall reputation in the community. If we bring clients through a home and things are left amiss, this will come back on us with the listing agent. When attending showings, leave the house how you found it. If the lights were off when you arrived, turn them off when you leave.

- Read the internal (non-public) remarks in the MLS! The listing agent has taken the time to share things with you about the property and the expectations associated with showing it.

The internal remarks are where basic requests or important notes, like whether or not the seller is permitting shoes to be worn in the house, are listed. The bottom line is that it's key to take the time to read this section—it'll save you, and all parties, a lot of avoidable headaches and is simply proper etiquette.

SOCIAL MEDIA DO'S AND DON'TS

This is clearly subjective, but over time, you will determine your personal preferences and best practices. As a baseline, it's a good idea to keep your posts as professional as possible. Which means it's probably not the best for business to use your Facebook account to debate politics or religion. If your social media is raising people's blood pressure, chances are it won't simultaneously be generating solid leads that convert to income.

Regardless of what you decide works best for you and your personality, here are a few basic tips, tricks, and rules to follow:

- Use social media as a tool to build your name, reputation and brand. There are many sites you can use to create content, as well as auto-post or have someone help you do it all. A few are:

  https://www.planoly.com/

  https://www.canva.com/

  https://www.fiverr.com

  https://www.upwork.com/

- Posting about your successes online can generate business within your inner circle. In addition to successes you have with buyers or sellers, it's wise to post positive client reviews or about upcoming fun events in your town. In the beginning, post about the classes you're taking and what you're learning. This is your building time—share your knowledge and build others' confidence in you.

- Rotate your posts on your personal social media platforms as follows; two or three personal posts, then one business-related post.

- Definitely have business pages on each platform, but know that people will also want to have access to your personal page.

- While we're on the topic of social media, consider that maybe, just maybe, it's a good idea to refrain from posting provocative pictures since right now your focus is wanting others to believe in you as a professional. Not to mention, this is a dangerous job and no one needs to invite attention from creepy stalkers. Be conscious of what you post and limit polarizing topics.

- We all have opinions on issues of all kinds; however, now that you're utilizing your social media platform to attract business, it's best to tone it down. For every issue, assume half of your followers are likely on one side and half on the other. Unless you really want to alienate half of the people following you, keep it off your social media platforms.

- Join as many real estate pages as you can—especially ones that offer referrals. Every day, multiple posts will be made by people looking for an agent in specific towns and states. Make sure your notifications are turned "on" and check the pages multiple times per day. In addition to replying to comments on the post, it can be beneficial to message or text the agent directly and let them know why you should be their go-to agent for that town.

BUYER'S AGENT-SPECIFIC TASKS

As a buyer's agent, you'll be going on a journey with a person, couple or family to help them figure out and find what they want or need. No sales or bullshit is needed. It's important to listen to them and do your best to get what they're looking for at a price that fits their budget, and then take on the stress while guiding them along the journey to the closing table.

That said, it's also important to study and watch the overall geographic area you cover. Understanding your market, pricing, location, available amenities, laws and restrictions will give you an advantage over other agents that don't have that same level of understanding. This knowledge will also instill confidence in you from prospective clients.

For example, if your town doesn't allow short term rentals (STRs), but you're working with an investor who wants to rent a property as a STR for income, familiarity with any relevant limiting restrictions would not only be beneficial, but arguably mandatory. The knowledge necessary to assist clients in purchasing, selling and leasing properties comes from extensive research and paying attention to your area. Watching the MLS will also keep you in tune with what is new on the market as well as keep you familiar with what prices properties in a specific neighborhood are selling for, how many days homes are on the market for, whether or not there are price drops and so on. If asked, you should know whether or not homes are closing above or below asking price, and if so, by what percentage. There are certain things in life where faking it until you make it works—area knowledge is NOT one of those things. Do your homework and pay attention.

Buyer's agent responsibilities

- Gathering a list of the desired features in a property that are important to your client/customer, such as the quantity of bedrooms, quantity of bathrooms, size of the house, style of the home, location, lot size and number of levels, will better aid you in finding them what they want. Knowing if they are open to paying homeowners association (HOA) fees is valuable information as well. Listening to your client and developing their list of "must haves" and "wants" will assist you in narrowing down the options for them to view.

- Understanding your clients financial situation will allow you to refer them to a trusted lender and be sure to only suggest properties that are in their designated price range.

- Set clients up on auto send MLS searches so that you will both be notified via email when homes come on the market that match their parameters.

- Once properties fit your clients parameters and they're ready to view homes, you will set up the appointment(s) and take them on showings. Some clients will view one property, and some may view dozens. It's an honor to be able to show them and help them get a better idea of what they really want, but let's also be real here—at the end of the day you are working for free until they find something and close on it. Be sure to take them to properties that are in their price range and have the amenities they most want.

- When showing a property, it's important to allow enough time to get there, unlock the door and turn on the lights—you want it to be ready for their arrival. While showing the property, look for any obvious issues, like cracks in the drywall and foundation and water stains on the ceiling.

- Always review the seller's property disclosure prior to going to the property so you have a sufficient understanding of the property and are ready to field any questions they may have. It's important to let them know the age of the heating and air systems if applicable, roof, septic, and leach field. Let your client know how long it has been since the systems of the home were serviced.

- When your buyers find something they want to purchase, you will walk them through the legal documents and make sure they understand what they are signing (believe it or not, people sign stuff without reading). Craft the offer, get signatures and present the offer.

- You will negotiate on your clients behalf and hopefully go under agreement.

- Once you go under agreement, you will oversee inspections, possibly more negotiations and communicate with and oversee affiliates, who are the other cohorts we need to work with to make things happen: lender, title company, attorney, inspectors and possibly subcontractors, for example.

- Prior to closing, you will set up and attend the walkthrough, where you'll check to make sure the water works, there is no new damage anywhere, ensure the appliances, heat and air conditioning systems are working and generally make sure the home is the way your buyer expected to find it. If it isn't, you will need to navigate that with the list agent and come to terms or potentially delay closing. You should also be ready for the worst case scenario: your buyer refuses to close on the property and wants to walk away. These are all possibilities.

- If you have a successful walkthrough, you will be responsible for reviewing the closing statement to make sure all the numbers look correct, reviewing the new deed, checking the spelling of your clients' names and making sure the property information is correct.

- If all that goes according to plan, you may "pass go" and move towards closing!

BUYERS: TASK CHECKLIST

01. CULTIVATE

WATCH LEAD

- [ ] Get Phone Number, Email Address, and Home Address
- [ ] Gather extensive notes on what they're looking for
- [ ] Update Database As Needed

NURTURE LEAD

- [ ] Follow-Up Call or Mailer from Initial Contact
- [ ] Put Buyer On Drip Campaign
- [ ] Send A Call To Action – Phone Call, Email, Direct Mail
- [ ] Check in: Did you receive the search I sent? Do you want to make any changes?

HOT LEAD

- [ ] Assist Buyer with Pre-Approval
- [ ] Compile List Of Properties To Show Buyer
- [ ] Daily Email or Text
- [ ] Set Up Buyer With A Buyer Tips Campaign

02. APPOINTMENTS

SCHEDULING INITIAL APPOINTMENT

- [ ] Is appointment for meeting and planning?
- [ ] Create and Send Meeting Agenda
- [ ] Prepare Buyers Packet & Marketing Information

INITIAL APPOINTMENT

- [ ] Send Reminder To Buyer for Upcoming Appointment
- [ ] Obtain Signature on Any Pre-Appointment Documents

CONTRACT APPOINTMENT

- [ ] Obtain Signatures on Agreements
- [ ] Submit Agreements
- [ ] Answer Questions

BUYERS: TASK CHECKLIST

03. ACTIVE

SEARCHING

- Search For & Compile Properties to Show
- Verify Availability
- Review Property Details/Documents
- Update Opportunity Details in Pipeline

SHOWING

- Set Up Times to Show Client Properties
- Schedule All Showings with ShowingTime or Agent
- Map All Properties for Best Route
- Confirm Meeting Location and Time with Buyer
- Take Notes During Showings & Update Files Afterward

NEGOTIATING

- Submit & Negotiate Terms of Offers
- Start To Add Offers Into the Opportunity Details
- Update Opportunity Details as Needed

04. UNDER CONTRACT

OPEN ESCROW

- Submit Contract
- Call/Email Buyer to Congratulate Them
- Send Buyer a List of Inspectors
- Send Buyer Copy of Contract & List of Important Dates
- Call/Email Buyer with Updates
- Have Seller Complete Any Required Docs/Orders
- Give Buyers List of Home Protection Plan Choices
- Confirm Earnest Money Deposit
- Coordinate Home Inspection Choice & Appointment
- Confirm Clients Have Received Escrow Package
- Confirm Delivery to Escrow Package
- Call To See If There Are Any Requests From the Lender
- Prepare Greensheet/Commissions (within 48hrs of eff. date)
- P&S and Client Contact Sheet to Title

BUYERS: TASK CHECKLIST

04. UNDER CONTRACT

INSPECTIONS

- Assist Buyer (If Needed) to Set Up Inspections
- Obtain Disclosures from Seller & Buyer
- Remove Inspection Contingencies Review
- Review & Approve Prelim
- Confirm w/Listing Agent when Inspections are Scheduled
- Review & Approve Termite Report
- Obtain Inspection Report
- Complete Escrow Instructions
- Post Inspection Negotiations & Draft Addendum
- Confirm All Dates
- Check All Documents Are in & Submitted

APPRAISAL / FINANCING

- Lender Sets Up Appraisal with List Agent & Seller
- Confirm w/ Lender Appraisal is Ordered
- Confirm Appraisal is in @ Value
- Obtain Inspection & Disclosure Contingency Removals
- Submit Home Protection Plan Choice to Escrow
- Confirm w/ Lender There are no Outstanding Conditions
- Remove Appraisal & Loan Contingencies
- Verify Closing Disclosure is Correct
- Confirm all Dates
- Ask List Agent for Utility Companies Contact Info/Acct #'s
- Continued Follow Up with LA, Lender, Title Co. (weekly follow up with all parties)

CLEAR TO CLOSE

- Make Sure There are no Outstanding Items With Escrow
- Verify Home Protection Plan has been Ordered
- Schedule Final Walk Through
- Remind Buyers to Turn on Utilities
- Coordinate Possession & Keys for Buyer
- Ready Gift and Card for Buyers
- Double Check all Docs are Uploaded and Submitted
- Submit Request for Payment at Table (if applicable)

BUYERS: TASK CHECKLIST

05. CLOSED

FINAL CLOSING TASKS

- Update Database
- Update/Finalize Opportunity Details in Pipeline
- Create/Order "Just Sold" Marketing Pieces
- Get A List of Closest 100 Homes from Title
- Put "Just Sold" Sign In Front Yard
- Set Reminder to Take Down Just Sold Sign after 2 Weeks
- Get Photo In Front of House w/Buyers
- Post Photo w/Permission of Buyers
- Deliver Gift to Buyers
- Send Thank You Card to Listing Agent
- Ask for Referral / Testimonial
- Setup Schedule for Client Follow-Up After Close
- Check MLS for Closed Listing Status & Upload to Compliance
- Add all Closing Documents and Submit to Compliance
- Put on calendar to check in with buyer in 7 days

HOW TO HANDLE INSPECTIONS AS THE BUYER'S AGENT

Inspections are important to oversee for or with your clients. Sometimes it can take an hour, other times it might be four or five hours, and by then, you're starving and want to scream. But regardless of how long it takes, it's important to stay patient throughout the duration of this critical part of the process. If a client shows up with over a hundred written questions for the home inspector and keeps interrupting him/her, take a deep breath, and allow the process to unfold. After all, it's part of the job! The buyer is spending their hard earned money on this home and has hired and paid the home inspector, and this is their time to get answers and understand the home. The focus of the inspection should be the structure, safety items and deferred maintenance, not paint colors. Oftentimes, clients get focused on cosmetics and it is our responsibility to redirect them to the important items.

What to look for and ask during the inspection process

Mechanicals

- If the property is heated by propane, ask if it was ever heated by oil. You will want to know if there are any current or past tanks in use or not in use on the property, including buried tanks.

- The heating, ventilation and air condition (HVAC) system should be fully operational. It would also be wise to ask for a service record.

- When checking the electric panel, it needs to have a door on it and be sure to note anything that seems out of place with the wires, or if anything is duct taped. Additionally, be aware of whether or not there is a Federal Pacific Electrical panel in the house, as these are known to be dangerous. When breakers trip, they can overheat and catch fire. Also, a home with knob and tube wiring (originally from the late 1800's) should not be used and lenders will typically not finance.

- All exhaust fans should be vented to the outside.

Exterior

- How old is the roof, what type is it and are there any issues? Hopefully the age of the roof is on the property disclosure, but often, the sellers have no clue.

- When inspecting the structural integrity of the chimney, the buyer can have the lining checked and may want to consider having a chimney sweep come out on inspection day. Chimney sweep companies are typically up to date on safety codes and regulations, making them an asset on inspection day. The buyer should ask the inspector or chimney sweep if there are any issues with the masonry or any corrosion or flashing issues.

- Gutters and spouts need to be checked because if they are not functioning properly, water could find its way in and cause damage.
- Check for negative grading, or spots where the earth slopes towards the structure, directing water into the home... You want the water to flow away from the home, otherwise it will find its way inside.
- If there is a well, clients can have it inspected. Typically, water quality testing will happen within the home, but the integrity of the system can be checked at the well.
- Septic systems handle the waste from the home and are expensive to replace so it is advisable to have a licensed contractor inspect the system.

Interior

- When entering the basement, look for any signs of past or present water intrusion. This will be notable by staining or sitting water.
- The foundation should be checked for any obvious signs of cracking or instability.
- Look for evidence of pests like mice, rats or wood eating insects. The damage and expenses that can result from pests can be great.

- Check for radon gas, if that's applicable to your area. Radon is an odorless, colorless and tasteless gas that is a radioactive carcinogenic. Testing requires the home to be closed up (no windows or doors opened) for 48 hours, and the test typically comes back in a couple of days. A number under four pCi/L is currently acceptable.

- In homes built before the 1980's, asbestos can be an issue. For example, it can be found in popcorn ceilings or in the exterior siding. It is best to check and follow the rules of your state when it pertains to asbestos, lead (prior to 1978) and other contaminants found and used in homes over the decades.

- Check the water pressure and make sure the faucets, showers and baths are working properly. If the water pressure isn't optimal, it can usually be fixed, but it's a good idea to have your client run the shower water to see if the pressure is to their standards.

- Appliances should be checked to be sure they are operational. For example, make sure all four burners work on the stove. You would be surprised how often one isn't working.

It's a good idea to pay attention during the home inspections. Ask the inspector for clarification on items he points out and take your own notes so that you can best explain everything to your client if they are not present. The home inspector will provide your clients with a report, but having notes in your own words is helpful when explaining the findings in the lengthy and overwhelming document. On this note, prepare your clients ahead of time about the report. Mention that the report will be lengthy (50 pages or more), extremely detailed and overwhelming. Let them know that you will go over it with them and point out what the main concerns are. Also, inform them that when a home inspector is inspecting a brand new home, they will still come back with a report filled with items—it's their job!

As the voice of reason and experience, make sure to always remain calm in all situations. It's easy for clients to panic since they are likely already stressed and anxious about all phases of the home buying process. It's our job to walk them through the process and be a problem solver. Your detailed notes could save a client from going off the rails on the emotion-coaster!

In 2020 and 2021, there was a massive reduction in the amount of inspections ordered due to buyers making their offers as contingency-free as possible. This was the result of the frenzied market conditions brought on by Covid which resulted in an intense and highly competitive bidding war environment, driving prices up and contingencies, like home inspections, down. In 2022, more buyers ordered inspections, but many were with the caveat of them being for informational purposes only, or up to a specified dollar amount. For example, a buyer might order an inspection, but it won't lead to repair requests or additional negotiations unless the total cost of any potential issues exceeds a specific amount.

WHAT TO CHECK ON A FINAL WALKTHROUGH PRIOR TO CLOSING

This is a very exciting moment for your buyer client, as they get excited anytime they have the opportunity to go back to their home-to-be. During the walkthrough, which usually happens within 48 hours before closing, you will walk around the property with your client, checking to make sure it is how they expected. If your client is busily focused on measuring spaces for furniture, you can have a checklist handy to go over on their behalf, bringing potential issues to their attention.

I've shown up to walkthroughs and have found water damage, forgotten food, furniture and even an abandoned pet. Oftentimes, the seller thinks they are doing the buyer a favor by leaving items behind, but this is rarely a blessing. Hey, maybe you could even start a comedic side hustle sharing the stories from your real estate job!

Things to focus on:

- Make sure the home is as the buyer client anticipated.
- Check to ensure all light fixtures are working properly.

- Check every faucet and shower to be sure the water is working, pressure is sufficient and that there are no leaks. Also, make sure the toilets are in working order.
- Test all appliances to make sure they are operating properly.
- Test the garage doors and make sure they open fully and close without issue.
- Open and close all doors and windows to ensure they are functioning correctly.
- Walk the property, check that the outside of the house looks as expected and that nothing is amiss.
- Make a list and take pictures of any issues if found.

Contacting the listing agent should you find any issues at the walkthrough is necessary so that you both have time to problem solve before the closing. In discussing the findings with the listing agent, some options are to push back the closing date in an attempt to give the seller time to remedy the problem(s), or ask for a credit to the buyer to compensate for the issues. Another option is to request an escrow holdback, which is when the attorney or title company holds back some of the seller's proceeds from the sale in an account until all items are deemed corrected and signed off by both parties. All of these options allow the deal to move forward, although the buyer has the right to cancel the deal if there isn't a satisfactory remedy.

THE LISTING AGENT'S FIRST APPOINTMENT WITH THE SELLER

The purpose of a listing appointment is to sit down with the seller, speak to them about their home, their use for a listing agent and their expectations. Typically, the seller will give the agent a tour of the home. This is a good opportunity to take diligent notes regarding the key features and systems of the property. Sharing the research that has been done on comps will lead to the pricing conversation. Property comps will help them understand the current market conditions and where their home fits into that.

While the market determines the going price range, some sellers feel their home is worth more because of what they have done to it or how meticulously they have cared for it. But unfortunately, not all home upgrades increase a home's value, and it's our responsibility to navigate these tough topics with our clients. Additionally, discussing commission fees can be a challenging topic, but if you want to get paid, it's another necessary conversation to have at the listing appointment. Stay confident and focus on the value you provide. Everyone wants a discount, but this is your moment to show them your negotiating skills! Negotiate for your full commission, whatever that might be to you.

The listing agent's responsibilities

Similar to the buyer's side, you'll want to know what's going on in your market. Knowing what's active, currently under agreement and closed is imperative to correctly pricing your listing. Counseling your client on pricing strategy is key, especially if they have an inflated sense of the value of their home. While navigating conversations with a client who feels their home is worth more than it actually is can be an art, it's always helpful to remember that this is their home and they likely love it the way it is, clutter and all. During your conversation with them, attempt to understand their motivations and goals, as this will directly impact the pricing strategy.

Familiarize yourself with expired listings, as they can be good indicators of over-priced properties. Contrary to expired listings, withdrawn and terminated listings are not necessarily due to being overpriced, but instead, could mean that the seller changed their mind about selling or terminated the contract with the brokerage for another reason. This is important to the listing agent because it differentiates between seller's motivation and pricing. Additional responsibilities are:

- Going into the MLS and conducting a search using similar parameters to the home you might be listing is necessary to get a better understanding of current market conditions. Looking back one, three or sometimes even a year (depending on the market and your size town) is a solid place to start when determining the value of a seller's home.

- Taking notes on the home's key features like the type of flooring, number of rooms or any upgraded finishes and the age of mechanical systems and roof will benefit you when you need to build out the MLS listing sheet. Additionally, make notes of things you think the sellers could do to help the property show better, like removing personal photos, decluttering, painting and repairing anything they're able to. Make sure to explain to your clients that this can translate to them getting a higher price. Providing them with recommended contractors takes a bit of the work out of it for them and increases the chance they'll make the call.

- Developing a marketing strategy and creating the flyers and ads is a fun and necessary part of the listing process. Don't forget social media!

- There are so many tasks that encompass our hefty list of responsibilities, from handling legal documents and arranging photo shoots and staging if applicable to setting up the appointments and completing the MLS input. Gathering documents such as the tax map, tax bill, tax card, and deed are also part of the listing agent's responsibilities.

- Scheduling open houses, if the seller is amicable to them, is not only a great way for you to show the property and sell it, but is also a fantastic way for you to acquire leads. Have a sign-in sheet at your open house and ask buyers if they are working with a buyers agent. If they aren't, you may have just got yourself a viable lead!

- Conducting showings, presenting offers, negotiating and communicating effectively and responsively with your client as well as other agents are additional responsibilities of a listing agent. As a listing agent, it's also your job to help your client arrange an attorney or title company for deed preparation, gather home utilities information for the buyer side and be available for appointments in your client's home.

- A listing agent may help their client by arranging movers, cleaners and contractors.

- As a listing agent, your goal and focus should be getting your client to the closing table with as little stress as possible.

LISTING AGENT-HOW TO HANDLE INSPECTIONS

While the inspection is for the buyer and their agent representative, you can be astute and potentially gain a better understanding of what details the report will include and what the buyer may ask of the seller. It's always good to get ahead of something if you can. You may also have information about the systems of the home that the buyer, their agent and inspectors could use some help with. After all, as the list agent, you should know the property better than anyone else, not to mention you'll likely have the owner on speed dial. By not being present when issues arise, the buyer and their agent are left alone to be frustrated or concerned without anyone to keep heads calm and solution-focused, which can translate into a deal collapsing.

LISTINGS: TASK CHECKLIST

O1. CULTIVATE

WATCH LEAD
- Get Phone Number, Email Address, and Home Address

NURTURE LEAD
- Follow-Up Call: Ask "How are you doing?"
- Put Seller on Drip Campaign
- Send a Call to Action – Phone Call, Email, Direct Mail
- Calendar Reminder: Check back in 7 days & Ask a Status Question to Re-engage

HOT LEAD
- Contact Seller to Schedule Listing Appointment

O2. APPOINTMENTS

SCHEDULING INITIAL APPOINTMENT
- Update Database
- Update Opportunity Details
- Create Listing Folder
- Create Listing Presentation
- Create/Find Comps

INITIAL APPOINTMENT
- Send Reminder to Seller for Upcoming Appointment
- Obtain Signature on any Pre-Appointment Documents
- Map out a Plan Together; Repairs, Staging, Timeline

CONTRACT APPOINTMENT
- Obtain Signatures on Agreements
- Submit Agreements
- Answer Questions

POST APPOINTMENT
- Submit Listing Docs Within Appropriate Timeframes
- Order Preliminary Title Report
- Follow-Up with Client – Provide Tips for Selling
- Take Photos with Phone
- Thank the seller for their time (Text or Email)

LISTINGS: TASK CHECKLIST

03. ACTIVE

PREPARE LISTING

- [ ] Send Copy of Contract to Seller
- [ ] Clean Up House
- [ ] Stage House
- [ ] Gather all Documents – Deed, Card, Bill, etc.
- [ ] Compose Ad Cop
- [ ] Start Creating Listing on MLS
- [ ] Get Photos From Photographer
- [ ] Input Listing and all Docs into your Brokerage's System

PUBLISH LISTING

- [ ] Put Up "For Sale" Sign
- [ ] Upload Pics (all websites)
- [ ] Publish Listing on MLS
- [ ] Create Flyers
- [ ] Create "Just Listed" Graphics for Social Media
- [ ] Post "Just Listed" Graphics
- [ ] Update any Opportunity Details

SHOWING / OPEN HOUSE

- [ ] Schedule Open Houses
- [ ] Update Seller on Marketing Efforts
- [ ] Email New Listing to Sphere
- [ ] Add Open House Leads to Database
- [ ] Add Hot Buyer Leads to Buyer Opportunity
- [ ] Create Social Media Ads
- [ ] Follow Up on Buyer Leads

NEGOTIATING

- [ ] Price Reduction?
- [ ] Change Price on MLS (if applicable)
- [ ] Add Received Offers into the Opportunity
- [ ] Compare Multiple Offers for Seller
- [ ] Create Offer Comparison to Seller
- [ ] Review Offers with Seller
- [ ] Send Counter Offers
- [ ] Accept an Offer
- [ ] Update Accepted/Rejected Offers in Opportunity

LISTINGS: TASK CHECKLIST

04. UNDER CONTRACT

ESCROW

- Congratulate / Call / Email Seller!
- Send Copies of Contracts & Important Dates to Seller
- Update MLS (Under Contract) within 48hrs of Effective Date
- Seller Complete Disclosures
- Prepare Commission Statement
- Have Seller Complete any Req'd Docs/Orders
- Order any Appropriate Docs
- Submit Escrow Deposit Form to Office (if applicable)

INSPECTIONS

- Update Seller with Inspection Date & Times
- Review Inspection or Request for Repair
- Negotiate Repairs/Credits
- Present and Have Amendments Signed
- Order any Additional Documents

APPRAISAL / FINANCING

- Update Seller of Date/Time of Appraisal
- Confirm Appraisal Value
- Clear Appraisal Conditions
- Remove Appraisal & Loan Contingencies
- Do We Have Loan Commitment?
- Continued Follow Up with BA, Lender, Title Company (weekly follow up with all parties)
- Give BA utility companies and acct #'s if applicable

CLEAR TO CLOSE

- Schedule Closing with Title
- Remind Seller to Switch Off Utilities
- Order Client Closing Gift!
- Ready Marketing Materials for "Just Sold" Announcements
- Request EMD Funds (7 days prior to closing date)
- Double Check that all Docs are Uploaded and Submitted for Review by Brokerage Compliance Department
- Submit Commission Statement and any Fuel Prorations to Title/Closing Company (7 days prior to closing)
- Request Payment at Table (7 days prior to closing)

LISTINGS: TASK CHECKLIST

05. CLOSED

FINAL CLOSING TASKS

- Update MLS & Database (within 48 hrs of closing)
- Add People Involved in Transaction to Database
- Upload Closing Docs and Submit for Compliance
- Take Sign Down from Listing
- Deliver Closing Gift to Seller
- Send Thank You Card to Buyer's Agent
- Ask for a Referral / Testimonial
- Setup Client Follow-Up Schedule for Seller

THE MULTIPLE LISTING
SERVICE (MLS)

Being thorough when entering property information will make it easier for agents and potential buyers to understand the property. Uploading documents and providing listing information is in the best interest of your seller, buyer agents and buyers. This is not an area to be lazy in, although you will see plenty of "lazy listings" on the MLS. With seller approval, provide the property disclosure, tax card, tax map, tax bill, deed, any restrictive covenants and when applicable, association bylaws, rules and regulations, meeting minutes and budget. Check your state rules for what is required to be uploaded into your listing.

Be sure to also include selling points in the community, such as if it's close to a specific point of interest or town center. When you're at the property, break out your phone, click on Google Maps and plug in spots of interest to see how close they are. This will allow you to add into the description that the ski mountain is a 12 minute drive, or the ocean is a 10 minute walk. You get the idea! You want to INFORM the consumer and highlight the positives, not bore them to death with meaningless information.

TASKS FOR AN OPEN HOUSE (OH)

Open houses are an opportunity for buyers to view a listing without a set appointment time. Typically the list agent will advertise a two or three hour window when the home will be open to the public to view and walk through and ask questions.

While you'll get into your groove and eventually figure out what you like to have on-hand at your open houses, here is a good starting point.

Items to consider having for an open house

- Open house signs
- Balloons
- Sign-in sheet
- Property documents
- Pens
- Business cards
- Snacks and drinks
- Shoe booties
- 9-volt batteries
- Trash bag
- Dog poo bags

Before the day of your open house

- If your MLS has OH announcements, get your day(s) and time(s) updated so it will automatically alert consumers and provide the hours and days of the open house. I'd suggest updating the MLS with the OH information a minimum of three days prior.

- Ask the lender and title company if they want to sponsor your open house and be present for potential buyer leads.

- Be sure to approve the time and day of the OH with your seller.

- Prepare to advertise the OH through social media, your website, agents within your office, agents within your local Board of Realtor® and nearby agents. If you're located near a state border, it might be worth marketing in both states.

- You can also create flyers and go door-to-door in the neighborhood. When going door-to-door to spread the word about your OH, ask the neighbors if they know of anyone who might be interested in buying. This is a great way for them to potentially pick their new neighbors and for you to receive new business.

- If there is time, posting an OH announcement in your local newspaper or at local businesses can help you get the word out and bring the most attention to the seller's property. You can even leave flyers at other brokerages to help generate traffic.

- Have a sign-in sheet and pens at your OH so that you can obtain a contact list of those who attended. A contact list is

85

important because if the buyer isn't working with an agent, that is a lead you can capture and potentially become their buyer agent.

- Let the seller know to remove valuables from the home before the OH.
- Having listing packets of property information and disclosures is something that should be prepared ahead of time. You can even set up a QR code so all the documents are readily available and in one place.

What to prepare for the open house

- Strategically place signage on roads leading to the house, or on highly trafficked streets so that potential buyers can find the property easily. You can tie balloons to your signs to draw more attention to them.
- Turn on the lights and open/unlock the doors to areas you want people to see.
- Make sure you know what the seller's rules are, like whether or not they allow shoes in their home.
- Some agents like to have bottled waters and ready-to-go snacks at their open houses, while other agents do full-on catering. Really, the point here is you have the freedom to get creative to ensure your open house is a welcoming and fun environment for potential buyers. While at the open house, don't sit on your phone or stalk people while they view the

home. This creates a pressured, uncomfortable environment for potential buyers.

- DO greet everyone upon entering and ask them to sign in and tell them a bit about the home, including any notable features that make it unique or desirable. Let them know you are available for any questions.

What to do after the open house

- Immediately after the open house, turn off all the lights and check that all doors and windows are closed and locked before leaving. Look around for anything that isn't how the sellers left it and tidy up accordingly. You will want to clean up any trash, snacks, documents, etc.
- On your way out of the neighborhood, take down your signs and balloons.
- Reach out and thank those who came for stopping by and ask them if they have any questions or if they can provide any feedback that can be conveyed to the sellers. If they are NOT working with an agent AND are not interested in the home, ask if you can help them find one more suitable for their needs. It is a good idea to include the property address and a picture of the front of the home in the correspondence so the recipient can easily identify the property you're referring to. If the buyer is working with a buyer's agent, it is appropriate to reach out to that agent and thank them for sending their client to the OH. It can also be beneficial to ask

them if they have any feedback on the property that can be relayed to the seller. Reach out to everyone on the same day as your OH. Waiting multiple days lessens the chance you will receive a response, feedback or the opportunity to work with that new lead.

HOW TO COMPLETE A COMPARATIVE MARKET ANALYSIS (CMA)

A Comparative Market Analysis (CMA) is a tool used to estimate the value of real estate by using other homes in the area to help determine the value of a seller's home. These are known as "comparables". Oftentimes, a seller will request an agent to provide a CMA prior to signing a listing agreement. It's a good idea to email the seller the listings of the comparables so they can sift through the pictures and data.

Once in the MLS, input the features of the home, such as the bedroom and bathroom count, square footage and year the home was built. When conducting a CMA, you will be searching for homes that have similar features to each other and you will utilize a "look-back" date by whatever timeline you decide. Play around with this feature to narrow down your search by the parameters of your choosing, within a specific timeframe you're interested in seeing.

In addition to market conditions, your specific geographic area will also make a difference when it comes to home value. Sometimes in rural areas, a real estate agent may need to expand the search radius to include other towns and limit the home factors (like not worrying about adding in the bathroom count) so that enough options populate in the search.

The amount of time a listing has been live on the MLS, known as days on market (DOM) and the outcome of that listing are also important factors to consider. Take note of expired listings of similar homes when preparing your CMA. If a home was listed for an extended period of time without selling, that's a good indicator that it was priced too high. Similarly, check how many days an under-contract home was on the market before going under agreement. This provides valuable information about the level of demand and how accurately the home was priced at that time. Closed properties directly show us what the seller was able to get for their home. Really take the time to review the properties and the pictures so you have a good idea of whether or not you are comparing apples to apples.

NEGOTIATION SKILLS

Always lead with what is best for your client and don't provide more information than necessary. And above all, DO NOT FABRICATE any details. For example, a friend of mine was buying a new construction condo and the list agent told him there was no limit on how many cars an owner could park, she also mentioned there would be an outside shower area as the condo complex was across from the ocean. NONE of the items turned out to be true once he moved in. Needless to say, he has a poor opinion of that agent in addition to being frustrated with his new purchase. Your job is to present the true facts, advocate for your client and get the best deal possible while clearly communicating and understanding their expectations.

In negotiations, remember that everyone wants the same thing: happy clients at a closing table. In order to achieve that and maintain a semblance of professionalism, don't text or call in offers to the listing agent—an offer is only valid in writing. This will save everyone from miscommunication and lots of potential headaches. It's also always a good idea to consult with your broker regarding expectations and do's and don'ts as well as having meaningful conversations with your clients so you fully understand their expectations. Managing expectations and maintaining clear concise communication are critical.

Do you want to really dive in and learn more about negotiating? Here are some titles to search on Amazon!

1. Negotiating Real Estate Strategies by Mark Furguson
2. Never Split The Difference by Michael Kramer
3. Getting to Yes: Negotiating Agreement Without Giving In by Roger Fisher, William L. Ury, and Bruce Patton

PROPERTY DOCUMENTS AND WHERE TO FIND THEM

The town is your friend for all property-related documents like the property tax card and deed. Depending on the area of the country you live in, these may be easier to retrieve than others. Some towns have everything online so you can easily download for free, while other towns will allow you to download documents at a cost. Others will have you go in person and retrieve a hard copy, possibly for a fee. Being familiar with the following documents and understanding not only what they are but what information is contained within them is necessary.

Deeds

Deeds can be found at the Registry of Deeds, which is usually accessible online. Typically, title companies you frequently use will send a deed over at no charge. Deeds let you know who owns the property and gives specific lot measurement and layout details as well as restrictive covenants that run with the land. A deed is defined by a book number, a page number and is signed, dated and a copy of it is recorded at the Registry of Deeds.

Property Tax Card

This document gives town specifics on the property. For example, it will include the bedroom and bathroom count, permit information, owner name, assessing amount, etc. This document is a good source for information and can be found at your local town assessor's office or on your county or state site.

Tax Maps

Tax maps are useful because they show you the basic layout of a parcel/property lines. Please note that surveys typically trump tax maps, as surveys are more specific and tax maps are general. Tax maps can be found on your town assessor's website.

Tax Bill

Viewing the tax bill will provide the current property tax amount billed as well as to confirm that the owner's account is not in arrears. Property tax bills can be found on your local tax collector's website.

Septic plans

Septic plans will show the original layout of the system as well as dimensions and location of all parts pertaining to the system. To retrieve the plans, check with the owner first, then check with the town or the Department of Environmental Services.

BEING INTENTIONAL ABOUT YOUR MONEY AND TAX DEDUCTIONS

Being intentional about your money is important as an independent contractor because the expenses are constant and the income is not. Utilizing a program to assist with the organization will be beneficial, as expenses will come at you quickly. The bottom line is that this is a unique career choice with a lot of expenses and unpaid work up front, making it quite challenging for a lot of new agents. Nothing much is free these days, budgeting and saving become your lifeline to sanity.

Brokerage monthly transaction fees, administrative and agent referral fees and desk rent are all business expenses you should be tracking. National, state and local expenses are different, so be sure you're aware of what they are for your area, how much they are in addition to when they are billed. These are all part of the cost of doing business.

Some expenses you may encounter and itemize for possible tax deductions

- Car-related expenses such as gas, tires, maintenance, repairs, insurance, payments, mileage, tolls and Mile IQ or equivalent. Deciding to paint your car some super cool color is not a tax deductible expense; however, if you decide to wrap it with your face and contact information, that will work!

- Common items you will need to have on hand at all times are a computer, printer, toner, paper clips, pens, folders, files, staples and markers, lock boxes, paper and ink—lot's of it.

- Advertising for listings and open houses and maintaining a supply of balloons, helium tanks, ribbons, snacks, bottled waters will help keep you prepared for a last minute open house event.

- Photography of properties is an expense that you will need to factor in when you have listings. Additionally, you may also want to include drone footage, aerial photos and videography, if your budget allows, in order to help showcase a property for the seller.

- Transaction coordinators generally get paid when a property closes and typically cost $300-$500 per transaction.

- Referral fees paid to other agents are an expense that is deducted from your commission at the closing table.

- A cell phone helps you to be readily available to potential and existing clients.

- Having Wifi in your car will allow you to respond to emails and do other computer work while you have down time between showings/meetings/etc.

- If you work from home, check with your accountant about prorating the expenses of your home for the square footage of your office. That could include all home-related things like heating, plowing, electricity, phone, Wifi, wood if used to heat your home, pest control services, water, sewer, etc.

- Marketing and advertising can be the biggest expense each year, but being as the job is to help clients sell homes and promote ourselves, that comes with the territory! Postcards, postage, boosted social media ads, business cards, signage, banners, sign frames, client gifts, stationary, cards, paid leads, advertising properties, logo apparel, newsletters, professional printing and lead generation are a few expenses you will come across that fall under the marketing category.

- Apps and programs such as Canva, REProphet, Mailchimp, White Pages, Folio, Microsoft Office, website hosting, QR generator, Squarespace, Google Workspace, Supra, Truthfinder and Forewarn are used in many aspects of the job and many have a fee attached.

- Educational courses and seminars are mandatory, and many are at a financial expense to you.

- Coffee and meals with clients can be fun and productive, but also cost you money.

It can take months to receive your first compensation check from your brokerage. For example, if you put a home under contract today and the buyer is financing the purchase, it could be as little as 30 days to closing or as much as 60 days, depending on several variables. Plan ahead and be prepared.

Once you get your first check, you might be tempted to use it to pay off your debt or throw a big party with flowing beer or champagne with your buddies to celebrate, but proceed with caution! While chipping away at that debt is important and celebrating your big achievement is fun, make sure you prioritize paying Uncle Sam's portion— April 15th is an important date to remember! One way to ensure you have enough money set aside for tax day is to immediately deposit the appropriate taxed percentage into a separate bank account each time you receive a commission check. This will serve as a reminder that, even in emergencies, this is absolutely not your money. If done properly, once all your expenses are calculated, you might even get to give yourself a tax refund!

Consistency in expense tracking will make life easier. Don't let it build up and think you will get to it at the end of the month or the end of the quarter. Inevitably, something WILL COME UP. You can simply use an Excel spreadsheet, Quickbooks or a service like REProphet, which offers automated web based bookkeeping, built for real estate agents by real estate agents. You can have your own dedicated assistant and meet with them weekly to stay up to date on your ROI and your P&L. They offer a free thirty day trial and a discount to our readers and members:

https://reprophet.com

Organization and self-accountability is a must! So dig deep and find a few minutes a day to keep up with your finances so you don't find yourself stressed and overwhelmed later. If you decide to work with an accountant, it's recommended you prioritize finding one as early in your career as possible so they can make sure you record everything they'll need come tax season. Starting with good record-keeping habits will save you from a shitload of stress later!

TIME MANAGEMENT

When planning your upcoming schedule and determining how many clients to take on, get real with yourself about what is and isn't realistic for you. We all get excited and pumped up about starting something new, and at times, can be overly ambitious about our plans. As independent contractors who aren't punching a clock, time management will help to set you up for success! No one cares whether or not you're doing your work and completing all tasks that come with being a real estate agent, but it will show when it comes to gaining and maintaining clients and a good reputation.

Making a realistic timeline to complete tasks can be helpful, as long as you stick to it. According to New York Times Bestselling author Kevin Kruse in his Huffington Post article titled, "Forty-one Percent of Tasks on To-Do lists Are Never Done," he suggests throwing away the to-do list since the list doesn't take into consideration how long a task takes to complete, nor does it distinguish a level of priority.

Instead, Kruse suggests scheduling it on your calendar. Everyone makes time on their calendar for important events and appointments.

When determining how to navigate the stresses of proper time management, consider what organization systems you'll use, how you'll keep yourself accountable and whether or not you'll be able to use your time productively, effectively, efficiently and intentionally.

Blocking time can be effective because you are deciding in advance what you'll do during specific times of the day. For example, you might decide to designate two hours each morning Monday through Friday for lead generation. If you put your important tasks on your calendar, they will likely get done. A critical component to time blocking is to control your environment by eliminating any distractions during your predetermined focus time.

Here are a few resources you can use to help you utilize time blocking as a method:
https://todoist.com/productivity-methods/time-blocking
https://www.betterup.com/blog/time-blocking
https://www.lifehack.org/881771/time-blocking
https://www.asianefficiency.com/our-podcast/
https://podcasts.apple.com/us/podcast/take-back-time-time-management-stress-management-tug/id1364141623
https://podcasts.apple.com/us/podcast/time-management-ninja/id1312677760
https://lauravanderkam.com/before-breakfast-podcast/
https://podcasts.apple.com/us/podcast/taking-the-time-to-define-your-bulls-eye/id1046485977?i=1000541361257

SETTING GOALS

Setting goals can help map out the trajectory of your career. As independent contractors, it's important to have a plan in place. Start by figuring out how much you HAVE to earn based on your total expenses. From there, decide if you can afford to be in real estate full-time or if you'll need a part-time job to cover your expenses until you build a stronger database. Keep in mind, your initial database is already in your phone and on your social media. So begin by reaching out to your existing contacts and let them know what you can offer them now that you're a real estate agent.

Once you know how much money you need to cover your personal and business expenses, you should take the time to understand what that means to you. For example, if you determine you need to net $100,000 annually, you will first need to figure out what an average home in your area sells for as well as the average commission compensation offered on homes in your area. It's always safer to use the lower numbers on both (sales price and commission price offered). So if the average home in your area sells for $400,000 and the average commission offered is 2.5 percent, you would gross $10,000 before expenses. But of course, once you factor in your expenses, the net amount won't be anywhere close to that, which is why it's important to have a firm understanding of all expenses involved. Granted, your expenses will change on each deal, but the point is you need to have an understanding of your unique situation so you can set your goals and figure out what you need to do to achieve them.

REALTOR® SAFETY

As a real estate agent, you'll be embarking on a career where your job is to do everything your mom and dad told you not to do! Accepting calls from strangers and agreeing to meet them at vacant homes is a big part of the job, and can potentially land you in some sketchy situations. And depending on where you live, you might not even have cell service when you arrive! Real estate can be an incredibly fun and rewarding job, but it's also important to recognize the reality of the situations you'll be in and prepare for any scenario that goes south.

Precautions you can take

At the beginning of my real estate career, I'd excitedly meet anyone to show them a home without asking if they were pre-approved to make sure they were serious ready to go buyers. Early one Saturday morning on a chilly New England wintery day, I received a call from a very excited buyer. He was super friendly and upbeat, and couldn't wait to see a particular home. Unfortunately, his work schedule didn't allow him the freedom to see the home until 7pm, nearly a week later. With each passing day he'd call and text with questions, always ending the calls with excitement about how this house was THE one, brimming with excitement. As our date approached, my gut was alerting me that something wasn't quite right with this situation. Thoughts of various worst-case-scenarios pulsed through my mind. I eventually decided to ask him for a copy of his drivers license, and mentioned that my brokerage "required" this. He canceled almost immediately and I never heard back from him again. This drivers license request has worked multiple times and while anyone serious won't mind, someone with ill intentions will probably not want to present a copy of their drivers license, hence creating a traceable record of communication and intention.

- Don't show a home to someone who you have only exchanged emails with—a verbal connection over the phone that provides tone can go a long way.
- Meet the buyer at a local coffee shop for the first meeting if you are part of a boutique brokerage without a brick and mortar office. This will keep things in public and safer than initially meeting at a property.
- Have the buyer send you a copy of their drivers license prior to the day of meeting and take the time to look them up online and check to see if they have a criminal record.
- It's beneficial to ensure someone from your office or even a family member knows where and who you are meeting.
- Be sure you park your car in such a way that you can't get blocked in.

- When showing a home, allow the customer to lead. Don't lead them up and down the stairs or get backed into a room.
- Don't go alone—stay alert and aware and have an agent join you whenever possible.
- Have pepper spray on you if it's legal in your area or a gun if you're licensed and that's your thing.
- Always listen to your gut/intuition.
- Consider taking a self-defense class.
- Take the Realtor® safety CEU course as there is valuable information within the class. Call NAR and check when the next course is.
- Have an SOS code in place with a friend/your brokerage. For example, call the office and ask them to pull the folder for the address you're at, and ask for a document inside. This will alert your friend/brokerage you want them to send the police.

You can check people out by using so many sites and apps. A few that are useful are Truthfinder, Whitepages (which has a reverse phone number lookup feature) and Forewarn, which is sometimes free through your MLS.

Resources for Realtor Safety from the NAR (National Association of Realtors) Site:
https://www.nar.realtor/safety/resources-for-personal-protection
https://www.nar.realtor/safety/56-safety-tips-for-realtors

https://www.nar.realtor/safety/putting-realtor-safety-first-course

Contact Andrew Hall at 312-329-8872 or safetycourse@realtors.org

GIFTING CLIENTS AND AGENTS

While giving gifts to clients or other agents can be a nice gesture, it is by no means mandatory. But, sometimes there's just something about the client or the agent that speaks to my heart and I get excited to go out and find them the perfect gift. When you do decide to give a gift, make sure it's personal! Branded bottles of wine or a personalized basket with local goodies can be good gifts, but the best ideas always occur when you let your feelings lead the way.

When giving alcohol-related gifts, PLEASE make sure they drink alcohol in the first place! For example, giving a bottle of wine to a client and then discovering they are a recovering alcoholic is a surefire way to create an awkward situation for the both of you.

It's a great idea to give gifts to agents who have referred clients to you. Send a gift and a card either after the deal has closed or in a bulk mail-out once or twice a year.

Some easy gift ideas are a hand-written card, nicely scented candle, wine, a gift certificate to a local eatery or coffee shop, a gift certificate for a home cleaning service or an in-home chef! Functional items such as a personalized address stamp, monogrammed champagne flutes, painting of their home, a gift basket with items from local vendors, an Amazon Echo or Ring Doorbell, a personalized front door mat, plant, flowers, or even a home warranty. This list is endless, but get creative and think about what the gift recipient might appreciate.

Visiting Etsy for fabulous gift ideas will give you loads of customizable gift options.

CUSTOMER RELATIONSHIP MANAGEMENT SYSTEMS (CRMS)

A customer relationship management (CRM) system is a multi-tiered system that allows you to input your leads and develop and build your database. A good CRM will take hours off your plate and keep you organized and connected. Of course, this will require you to input the information, know how to use it and follow through!

A good CRM will help to increase sales by keeping things organized and streamlined. Today's CRMs typically include marketing tools so you can set the system up to send emails, texts, post on social media, wish your client happy birthday or perhaps remind them that it has been ONE year since they bought their home! The CRM allows you to automate communications, which can go a long way in keeping you front of mind with your database!

Ask the company about set-up time and training and ask to see examples so that you can better gauge ease of use. You'll want to ask about tech support, as this will be critical to lowering your stress! What are their customer service or tech support hours? Cost will also obviously be a factor for you, and some can be super pricey! What can this CRM do for you? Get a list of features and check to see if there are basic features included or if you have to purchase them as upgrades.

Some CRM choices

- Rainmaker
- Pipedrive
- Freshsales
- Capsule
- Oracle Netsuite
- Brivity

Brivity is offering our readers and members a HEFTY discount on their cutting-edge technology with their all-in-one real estate CRM platform

IN CONCLUSION

Thank you for sticking with me. After reading all of this, you're ready to make your mark in real estate! Unless you're intentional and consistent about setting and keeping boundaries, your time isn't your own. But the trade-off is that your growth and income potential is only limited by your drive, effort and work ethic. Be a badass and put the effort in and make all that studying for the exam worth it! The truth is, it's thrilling to be able to help someone find and buy their dream home. And when you help someone get the highest amount of money possible for their home, even better! You'll meet so many people, make so many memorable relationships and potentially create wealth for your family at the same time. Moving forward, get comfortable being uncomfortable. If you remain humble, grateful, honest and ethical, you will go a long way.

I have your back—you are not alone. I, along with agents across the country, will be there for you and with you as we grow and spread the word about the existence of this guide and our community of support and encouragement for newbies and agents in need. I hope you'll join us and spread the word! I have downloadable forms, the REAL AF Tool Kit, Facebook public and member-only pages, online weekly member REAL AF online support group sessions, small group and even one-on-one chat sessions with me. Throughout the REAL AF online community you can stay connected and have a supportive and fun place to check-in.

My best to you!

Julie Chin (Jules)

QUOTES, ARTICLES CITED

Article: Kevin Kruse

To-Do Lists

https://www.huffpost.com/entry/forty-one-percent-of-tasks-on-to-do-lists-are-never-done_b_9308978

Article: Andrea J Stenberg

Rule of seven, marketing

519-377-3223

andrea@thebbe.ca

https://www.thebabyboomerentrepreneur.com/258/what-is-the-rule-of-seven-and-how-will-it-improve-your-marketing/

DISCOUNTS

YOUR
REALTY
LE√ERAGE

Recruiting | Training | Coaching
Consulting | Admin Services

Build A Sign is offering Real AF Program readers & members 40% off signs and free shipping! The code is:

REALAFBASRE40FS

The website is:

www.buildasign.com/eas/realestate